Out of My Mind

Late Night Contemplations About Trauma and Neglect

By Ruth Cohn, MFT

To all the Blog Readers who told me that my weekly musings mattered to them.

And to my dear friend Dawn who said "these should be a book!"

Sign up to Ruth's email list to receive a free digital copy of *Cycles of Escalation*. A brief eBook which explores how to manage triggers within relationships.

www.ruthcohnmft.com

Contents

01 / Isn't Transference Grand?

6

02 / Existence – Triggering, Pronouns
and Learning from Experience

12

03 / You Are My Kind

20

04 / Changing Spots

26

05 / The Journey of 1,000 Miles: Hallucinogen-Assisted
Psychotherapy for Trauma

32

06 / Trauma and Addiction: Reflections On
My 38 Years

37

07 / The Shape of Shame: Trauma, Posture and
Coming to Tall

40

08 / Too Much of Nothing: Spotlight on Neglect

47

09 / Waking Up to ACES – Neglect Edges into
Awareness

58

10 / George Floyd – Restitution, Apology and
Forgiveness

62

01

Isn't
Transference Grand?

Idealization, Idolatry and the Quest for Authentic Attachment

Early in my career, when I was in a post-graduate training program and just beginning to see clients, I remember when one of my first clients gushed hyperbolically about how wonderful I was. I was dazzled and delighted. "Maybe, just maybe I will be good at this!" I thought. When I proudly told my supervision group what she had said, a woman in my group, a year ahead of me in the program sarcastically retorted, "Isn't transference grand?!" I went silent, feeling deflated and ashamed. And although at the time I thought she was snotty and mean, I never forgot her words.

Transference is the projection onto the therapist of feelings for a real or longed for important other, commonly but not exclusively a parent. What my colleague was reminding me, or telling me, was "It's not about you, Dummy!" Also, we invariably come crashing down from the proverbial pedestal, to become worse than scum. I have since come to understand, how these projections can be some of the richest sources of information about a client's often unremembered past. Neglect leaves such gaping holes in interpersonal memory, that other media of communication than the spoken word become the requisite vehicle for the telling and reconstructing of personal narrative.

I remember one client telling me, "I really don't remember anything about other people. When I try to remember my childhood, I just see bushes, and maybe our various dogs." We slowly began to learn her story by studying her present relationships, and dynamics she did remember.

Idolatry

It is curious to me, that as I find with many of my neglect clients, although I have blank or spotty memory about my childhood, I have vivid memory of books. I remember from second grade Sunday school a picture from a Bible Story picture book of Abraham smashing the idols. We were learning the Ten Commandments and the concept of "One God." In Jewish synagogues there were to be "no graven images" meaning no images or statues of human subjects who might be attempting to upstage the One God. Abraham, in the picture, a young boy, not that much older than me, in his little toga with a stick thrashing the white marble statues to the sanctuary floor. I remember thinking this was very strange. The lesson was, we were not supposed to worship idols. Somehow I did not quite get it.

I was always a hero worshipper. I could not seem to find real people to connect to, I just did not know how. But I would create them out of some raw material that I found in the environment, and invent the relationships I did not know how to have. When I was about 12, my "first love" was Thomas Wolfe. He was an author who wrote mammoth 500-600 page novels, known to be autobiographical, where the protagonist was depressed, intense, insatiable, creative and desperately alone. Wolfe the writer died at 39. So even though he was dead, I believed I had found my match, he was like me, I was not the only one. Wolfe was from Asheville, North Carolina. It was on my bucket list to go to Asheville, see his home and the birthplace of all these stories that filled my world.

In 2012 I had the opportunity to go to Asheville for a Neurofeedback training. I was delighted! By now it was 45 years later. I had a different brain and a completely different relationship landscape, thankfully. I booked a hotel across the street from the Thomas Wolfe House, the boarding house Wolfe's mother ran, that featured in all the books; and where the real people had lived. I spent a day taking pictures of everything there.

In the gift shop I bought a little miniature of the marble angel made famous in the title of his book Look Homeward Angel; and a 560-page biography. After the training I eagerly devoured the biography in the same devouring way that Thomas Wolfe the man had related to most people and things. I learned from the biography, that he was a misogynist, he was an alcoholic, he was antisemitic, he was racist. What was I thinking? Who was that young girl?

I recently heard Bessel van der Kolk say, "idealization is a defense against terror." I was terrified that I was a different species, that there was never and never would be anyone like me. In my quest for a partner or twin, I had to make someone up. Wolfe was the clay. The void left by neglect is so gaping, it terrifies. We have to fill it with something besides bushes or book illustrations.

"Seremos como Che"

Idealization

In my twenties I became politicized. By then I had given up on being seen or known by my parents. My father's suffering and his hero story or overcoming his suffering and making a successful life, became the model. But I also was angry and rebellious. I wanted to get his attention and approval, but I also disavowed that wish. So, I chose something that would perhaps outrage or anger him. At that time democratic governments were tumbling all over Latin America, smashed by military dictators not unlike Hitler. I adopted an identity as freedom fighter, out to overthrow fascist rulers, and perhaps even die doing it. The ideal was Ernesto "Che" Guevara.

Originally from Argentina, Che grew up with privilege and became a doctor. But he sacrificed everything to be an internationalist fighter, who led the Cuban people to freedom and died doing it. Perfect! That was who I wanted to be. The new female version of Che. Ever trying to fill the empty void left by neglect, find an identity, a way to be like my father, but not too much. To be seen and known, respected and loved. And with luck to die doing it, a noble way to end the pain. I tried to do this and had a terrible psychological crash doing it, which ultimately led me to psychotherapy.

The child of neglect, lacking a mirroring other, has no self to be. I have shown Ruth Lanius's shocking brain scans of the child of neglect, whose brain is firing faintly if at all. The default mode network which is the home of the sense of self, is virtually missing entirely. "Without a self" as Lanius reminds us, there is no other. So we continue to create some version of relationship, but being distorted and alienating, they don't last. Like many survivors of neglect, I left a trail of relationship wreckage behind me, until I finally attached to a therapist, and stayed for many, many years. I am happy to say I now have very fulfilling and mutual relationships, a partner of 35 years, and dear friends. But I did not grow the circuits in the way we were designed to. That is the task that neglect leaves us with. And that is why we must learn to become the therapists that can heal this.

In Cuba I saw a billboard that said "Seremos Como Che," This means we shall be *like* Che. The emphasis is mine. We will aspire to emulate, but not to be him. The void of self is devastating. The tragic impact of neglect. Getting a spine, getting a voice, big tasks. And big tasks for the therapist to learn all the possible access routes to assist. We must also resist the temptation to buy into the inevitable projections, positive and negative, or even to recognize them when they occur. Another reminder of why the therapist who works with neglect, perhaps even more than any other therapist, must do their own personal work. We don't want to miss that boat like our clients' parents did!

Existence – Triggering, Pronouns and Learning from Experience

I worked at the San Francisco VA for one year to the day. It was March, 1989-1990. I remember it well because it was the year of the historic San Francisco earthquake. I was definitely not cut out for that work, but I definitely recommend that any trauma therapist do a stint at a VA as there is so much to be learned there. In 1989 there were still plenty of Vietnam vets cycling in and out. And yes I do mean cycling. It was a wacky system, I don't know if this has changed since then, but at that time, if a veteran recovered, or if PTSD symptoms even partially abated or remitted, their benefits were systematically cut. "service-related disability" was measured in percentages, and dollar amounts were proportionally calculated. So there was built in incentive to not get better. Of course we really did not have good treatments back then either.

One of the great lessons I in my time at the VA was about "triggering." Admittedly I try to avoid that term, preferring to use activating or stimulating old trauma. By definition, trauma re-sets the brain to ferociously defend the organism against letting the trauma happen again. So any stimulus even vaguely reminiscent of the trauma, can activate a cascade of sensory, emotional, body sensation or whatever that individual retained of the original experience. I don't like the word "triggering," because in my mind it conjures gun violence, which in many cases is accurate, but also in many cases not. In my work with traumatized couples, who activate one another quite readily, unfortunately, such language can sound accusatory in suggestive ways that can exacerbate conflict. However, it is hugely important to learn about this, and the veterans taught me well.

My most potent teacher was a man whose entire platoon was wiped out before his eyes by a helicopter bombing in Vietnam. All of his buddies were dead, and he was the sole survivor. The SF VA is in a beautiful location perched on the ocean. The view is serene. I remember one scenic afternoon a helicopter passing overhead in the blue cloudless sky. This man was instantly sent into a tailspin of abject terror. He was screaming as he rolled under the nearest bench shaking. It was as if it were happening right now. That particular helicopter chopping innocently by was benign, like an unthinking partner often can be. It was a dramatic depiction I will never forget.

The word "triggering" has also found its way into common parlance, where it is used to mean all kinds of things, even just generic unsavory emotion. I am very picky in its use as it has an important and precise meaning, whether or not we choose to use that term. I insist on precision as it is vitally important for healing, to learn when we are activated, or activating the other.

In couple's therapy, when one partner is activated and truly believing it was the other partner that upset them this much, I will routinely say something like, "... this feeling you are having right now, what does it take you back to from your childhood? Tell your partner a story about a little girl/boy who felt just like this." The point is to get to the original trauma material, that the partner is simply stimulating. The stimulus is not without merit, but it is a small proportion most of the time. This is an important lesson in both psychotherapy and couple's work.

In a session the other day, I was sitting with a lesbian couple. It was a calm moment, and one of the partners, a child of tragic neglect, bravely said to me "...There is something I need to say to you." I prepared myself. She said, "You know how you say, 'tell MaryAnn (not her real name of course,) a story of a little girl who felt just like this...' that really upsets me..."

I expected I knew why. Children of neglect are often frustrated by a gaping poverty of interpersonal memory. That is often the diagnostic marker that tips me off when I first meet a new person. They also generally have a hard time knowing what they feel. I expected this client's frustration with me, to be one of those, or both. I was humbled and surprised by what I heard instead. She said, "My mother always treated me like a little girl, dressed me up in girly clothes, made me get the girls' sneakers that wear out in three days, instead of the boys' Keds with the rubber caps. But I never felt like a girl. I did not exactly feel like a boy, but I definitely did not feel like a girl! I tried and tried to tell my mother this. She just ignored me, as she did about most things. I felt unheard and unseen, completely not known." (All classic traumatic markers of neglect.) And most decidedly "I felt like I did not exist!" And "when you say that to me, I feel again, like I do not exist!"

Needless to say, I was horrified! I could not believe I had made that terrible, ignorant mistake! Here I am supposed to be so knowledgeable about neglect, and more, I am a sex therapist! I had thought of myself as scrupulously mindful about sexist language, and issues of sexual orientation; I had thought I was sensitive and self aware about all things sexual. I felt terrible about my unthinking binary assumption. Much more than a "micro-aggression," it seemed like a "macro-aggression" if there is such a word. I fell all over myself apologizing. And I thanked her for educating me.

Although I am well familiar with the current discussion about pronouns, apparently not so much as I thought. I can see I really did not get it! Until now. I am immeasurably grateful! I am grateful that my client had the "spine" and the "voice" to tell me. By spine, I mean agency, or the ability to operationalize purposeful action on their own behalf. Voice, being the ability to express out loud and in relationship, what is genuine and authentic. These are the greatest tasks of healing from neglect.

I recently heard an interview with rock musician, Tory Amos. Certainly not any kind of fan of hers, I was driving and almost always tune in to Public Radio in the car. She apparently had just written a book, so that was nominally the focus of the interview. The interviewer asked her, "So how was it for you writing a book?"

Amos answered, "it was hard!"

The interviewer queried,

"—so, what was hard about it?"

Amos replied:

"My first language is music. Spoken word is my second language. It was like writing a book in my second language."

I thought, "how profound!" Something as seemingly elemental as language, is so easy to not think about. Easy because of cultural, ethnic, cisgender, able-bodied chauvinism, narcissism or sheer blindness. It is so easy to take for granted that the language in my head or tongue is the predominant or majority language. Particularly in a world of neglect, that is so solitary, it is so effortless, and actually one's default mode, to create one's own whole world, without even realizing it. My husband used to say with a laugh, "You mean you are not in my head?" He really was only half joking. It is so easy to just assume.

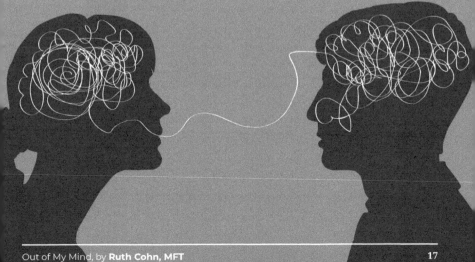

With gender as with race, culture and sexuality, bodiedness, age, so many categories, it is so important to watch our language. Oy vey! So many languages to learn. Alas it leads us back to the foundational missing experience, taking the time, having the care and the bandwidth to actually learn who a person is. With mindful attention, thoughtful presence... it seems so simple. And simple it is, but not easy. If only that simple ingredient were part of everyone's daily lexicon, and everyone's early experience, how much trauma and early life trauma would be eliminated? And without trauma, as Bessel van der Kolk so sagely proclaims, "The DSM would be a pamphlet!" Not to mention much of the menu of physical illnesses, whatever that manual is called. I was immensely grateful to this client for having the guts and the gumption as well as the articulateness to correct my sloppy delivery, and to teach me. I think it was a healing moment for us both.

Learning from Experience

One of the great gifts of the 1990's the "Decade of the Brain," was to learn that the brain is plastic. Ironically, that fateful year at the VA, rattled by the earthquake, also engendered that! We had previously thought we were born with a lifetime set of neurons, rather like our life's quota of ova should we happen to have female anatomy. That is what you get, we thought. We now know we can regenerate, and birth new neurons, and we can learn. Our dogs and other mammals can too, if we have the patience and generosity of spirit to teach them. What a blessing! We have more than one chance!

The brain can change, and even the mind! Neurofeedback is based on this principle in its very obvious beeping way: "operant conditioning." Psychotherapy as well, and none of us would engage in it unless we had some remote belief, at least some of the time, that change is possible. Of course in many cases we must do our part to make it happen. And in many cases we can. As the saying goes "Pray to God (if that is one's paradigm of course!) and keep rowing to shore."

Now it is my task to integrate what I have learned, to remember and make use of it, with this client, and in the world. My world is enlarged when I do, and how healing to others to be accurately seen and heard, not to mention my own pleasure in seeing the appreciation in the eyes and body of the other. Because we are designed for interdependence, the brain also kicks in a bonus reward of its own with a dopamine surge, for re-enforcement! More joy and love are in circulation. In this COVID-weighted world, so sorely needed. Can you beat that?

You Are My Kind

Neglect, Being Wanted, A Place to Belong

Some years ago, I was asked to be a main presenter at a weekend Institute of the American Association of Sex Educators, Counselors and Therapists (AASECT) to teach about trauma and sexuality. I was thrilled. It was my first time ever being invited in that public of a way. I was the main attraction and I could hardly believe it. The director of the program was a lovely woman named Susan whom I had never met before.

I was self-conscious about everything. I never missed a conference, but I had never attended one of the weekend "institutes" I did not really know my way around PowerPoint then, and I had endless nervous questions, while also being embarrassed about having so many questions. Oy vey! What I was soon glad to learn, was that Susan always answered my emails immediately, with patience, care, warmth, and never implying any kind of judgment or sense that my questions were excessive or reflected ignorance (-or idiocy which is how I felt.) I discovered that Susan was much like me: thorough, somewhat perfectionistic and painstaking to do her best. As ever, there is always a song in my head. I asked her "Susan, do you know the old song by Santana, "You Are My Kind?" I love that song, and I felt that very kindred, connected feeling with her. She said she did not know the song, so I sent her a youtube link so she could hear it.

Susan gently guided me through the preparation process for the Institute, and through the Institute itself. All went quite well. As the weekend drew to a close, I was more than a little relieved. Susan did one last amazing thing, that cemented the feeling that she is my kind, (and also brought me to tears.) As the weekend drew to a close and people filed out, she piped our song through the large conference room loudspeaker.

Affiliation

One of the tragic sequelae of trauma and neglect is the shame and grief ridden feeling of not belonging anywhere. The child roams the world orphan-like, like the mythical little bird in the famous children's book Are You My Mother? In that story, the poor little thing approaches every creature (and even some machines) in its path, asking the same urgent question: "Are you my mother?" It is a profound and primitive primal need to be attached to a caregiver and a pack, certainly when we are young and not nearly able to care for ourselves, but not only then. It is wired in to the limbic brain, that the first line of defense when a child or young mammal is scared or distressed is the "attachment cry." We reach for connection. Only after that fails, do we then resort to the fight/flight or freeze defense.   The need for affiliation, to be connected and secure by being part of a larger group, persists through the lifespan. When that connection is deficient or missing in early life, it can become, as for the little bird, a relentless and gnawing quest. For the child of trauma and/or neglect, the search for a group or family can go all sorts of ways.

I got very confusing messages growing up. My parents both being survivors of the Nazi Holocaust and refugees in the United States, felt on one hand, like strangers in a country that was not ours, while also being immensely relieved and grateful to be there. They felt both welcomed, and a profound fear and mistrust. We were supposed to fit in but not "assimilate" too much and lose our identity. And never quite let our guard down, because you never know when people will turn on you. It was a confusing message for a child. I surely did not know what that identity was. My father often told us "You just don't know what it is like to go to bed hungry, or live on bread and worms!" So, I knew I was not really like him, and did not know how to be enough like him to please him. My mother's first major heartbreak was when as a little girl, her best friend turned on her from one day to the next, to join the Hitler Youth, I longed, like all little girls, for a best friend. But not like that!

When the Need for Affiliation is Exploited, or Goes Awry

When I was in college, I became an impassioned political activist. Latin America was exploding with military coups and fascist dictatorships that were enough like my parents' experience as to make me feel perhaps kindred, but different enough, that I could rebel against my parents. I remember a book I read during that time, the story of a Chilean diplomat, Orlando Letelier, exiled by the dictatorship and living in Washington DC. He was murdered by a car bomb on Embassy Row in broad daylight. It was a chilling account.

Letelier's killer was identified, as Michael Townley, an American employed by the secret police of the Chilean Dictatorship. The book was largely a character study of Townley, or that is what I remember about it these 40 years later. Townley was a lost soul. He lacked a sense of direction, a sense of home and identity, roots or purpose. Somehow, he wound up in Chile. I don't believe the book told much of his background. But my experience has been, that whenever a young person travels thousands of miles from family and home, there is always a story. In Chile, he was prime bait for the Chilean DINA, the notoriously vicious and cruel secret police, best known for the torture of thousands after the 1973 coup. Being disenfranchised and searching, Townley was a ready and receptive candidate and rapidly excelled at the job. He was technically skilled, and efficiently orchestrated and executed the bold murder of Letelier and his young assistant Ronni Moffitt. Townley was a vivid example of the disconnected, rootless, most likely child of neglect, being easily seduced and transformed into a tool for some other and that other's personal agenda. So, in need of someone to please, and a grouping to be a part of, they can seamlessly become even a proficient professional killer.

at same time period in my life, one night
nent mate in Berkeley, brought home a
man she had encountered on the street.
-like woman was sobbing uncontrollably, and
blubbering unintelligibly, clearly under the influence
of some unidentified drug. She was terrified and
grief stricken, and probably no more than 18 at the
most. My friend found her curled up and shaking on
the sidewalk, in the vicinity of a "spiritual" cult there
dancing and chanting on Telegraph Ave. All we could
discern was that she had been lured to join them, and
drugged into this barely conscious state. We kept her
safe overnight, and in the morning when the drug
had worn off and she could talk, we learned that she
also, was a disenfranchised, survivor of some sort of
trauma, again, a ready target for a "group" or a place to
belong. I don't remember the rest, but just remember
making the connection with Michael Townley. How
deep and sometimes blinding the loneliness, longing,
the driving attachment need can be! It can over-ride
coherent judgement and land the child of trauma and
neglect (at any age) in some community or role, they
might never have chosen.

Climate Change

Although I always understood climate change as a
concern, it was never at the top of my hierarchy of
concerns. I was always most compelled by causes with
a more directly human cost and exhibiting palpable
human suffering- until I read Thomas Friedman's
book, *Thank you for Being Late*. The book is one of
those good books that are about 200 pages longer
than necessary, but I did soldier all the way through it.
In the chapter about climate change, it described how
in countries of East Africa and the Middle East, climate
change resulted in such drought and water shortage
as to kill whole crops. Farmers were desperate both to
make a living and to feed their families; and food was
in short supply. Due to climate change, people were

starving. And hungry people did not feel taken care of by their governments, like neglected children, they were left to fend for themselves. Many men began to migrate to other places where they might at least earn enough to feed their families. Many of course died. And many enraged by the neglect and by hunger, were readily receptive to terrorist ideologies and larger group identifications, spawned at that time. I can only imagine and guess, that those receptive to become terrorist killers and members of cultlike organizations, had an antecedent of neglect, an old rage ready to be ignited and erupt, and an urgent need for affiliation, activated by hideously neglectful governments. Again, what role might neglect play in dangerous or deadly dynamics we see in the world? These are questions that roll around in my mind.

The need to attach and belong is ubiquitous and primal. We share it with all mammals and some birds and invertebrates too. It is not to be underestimated in ourselves. Susan made me feel connected, cared for and like I mattered. That profoundly affected what I felt able to do, as well as my mood of joy and love through the process of preparing and delivering my presentation. All the more reasons why we must heal neglect, both positive and negative. Humans function better and feel better when they/we are part of something. And when we are not, our desperation can make us even perilously vulnerable. We can easily find ourselves in the "wrong" relationships, one way or another. We must be passionately present for our own children, and we must learn how to facilitate healing in the adult survivors of neglect and interrupt both the suffering and any intergenerational transmission.

Changing Spots

Mistakes, Butterflies and Potholes

I have a special affection for leopards. As I love to say, "you know the old adage 'A leopard can't change its spots?' Well, I can. And I change my spots every chance I get." Healing is all about that. The "Decade of the Brain" and neuroimaging technology taught us that "Neurogenesis" is possible, that we can grow new

neurons. Before that we believed we were born with our life's quota of neurons, and that was that. We now know that with neurofeedback, psychedelic assisted psychotherapy, somatic therapies, mindfulness practice, and yes even the old fashioned "talking cure," we can generate not only connections, ie networks, but molecules. This is wonderful news for all of us, both with respect to our own brains and our clients' brains if we are practitioners of some kind. So why do spots have such a bad rap?

I remember when I used to drink alcohol, I had to either stop wearing white, or switch from red to white wine. All my pretty white blouses were speckled with unsightly red spots. Oy vey, I always was a sloppy drinker. As an adolescent, ugly facial spots, we called them "zits," were referred to in commercials for acne products as "blemishes." Spots were blights on the skin, and on faces that in so many cases already housed shame and self-doubt, or self hatred. Spots were like nature's "mistakes." But nature, for the most part, does not make mistakes. If left to itself, it has a brilliant unshakeable plan. Occasionally there is an aberration or mutation, as with the Corona Virus for example, but perhaps we will ultimately come to discover what the ecological (or existential) intention of that was to be. Most likely it is human intervention that produces disasters of nature, or so is my jaundiced and not-research-based speculation.

Once I had the privilege to visit Milan, Italy. I admit, in my love for pretty things of many kinds, I love clothes. Milan is a wonderland as the fashion hub of the world. Of course, we had to visit the Armani showrooms, a veritable museum of haute couture, clothes I could and really never would buy, but love to look at like I love looking at art. I was struck by a theme, that in every window in a long seeming small city of windows, each of the numerous masterpiece garments, whether on a mannequin or a hanger, had a conspicuos wrinkle in the way it was hung or draped. It was striking. I wondered, "what is he trying to say?" My husband did not notice until I pointed it out. Was he trying to teach us something about "mistakes?"

"Mistakes"

Once in a training with the somatic therapy genius Peter Levine, we were instructed to make four "mistakes" in every practice session. It was an intentional part of the assignment. The idea was to integrate the idea that mistakes are inevitable in this work. And to develop the humility to tolerate and learn from them. And then to learn to repair them. So many of us who grow up with trauma and neglect, come to learn that mistakes can be life threatening, or have the "hubris" to strive to be "perfect," blameless or safe from retribution; or worthy of love. A futile aspiration.

In relationship, "mistakes" are an inevitable ingredient in development. The attachment researchers teach us, that even in the ideal secure attachment, where the attunement of primary caregiver and infant is "good enough," the optimal percentage of accurate attunement, the best we could hope for is 30%. 30%!! That means that the other 70 percent of the time is the delicate dance of rupture and repair, rupture and repair. That is how we learn about relationship, and really about being. How sad that in the world of trauma and neglect, these skills are rarely learned, so the inevitable ruptures are terrifying, even life threatening. And relationship comes to in effect be an icon for suffering, however much it is longed for.

Much like Peter, the attachment research people teach us that the "mistakes" of rupture are invaluable, and much better training than smooth sailing without rupture. As my husband exclaimed many years ago when we emerged from the nightmare of chronic cycles of triggering and reactivity, "Wow, knowing how to recover when we disconnect is such a relief! I don't have to worry so much about screwing up, because I know we can get back together if I do. I don't feel so chronically unsafe and fearful around you anymore!" What a blessing!

Potholes in Cuba

As long-time serious bicyclist, my nemesis became potholes. I have only had two serious crashes in my in my 50 plus year cycling life, and in both cases I lost consciousness, so I don't really know all of what happened. I admit, that I am grateful to have had those two traumatic events so I could experience different trauma modalities on those sorts of "one-time" incident traumas. What I did know was that I came out of the accidents with anxiety about bad road surface, and a veritable phobia of potholes.

Riding in Cuba, was like a dream come true. Just going there was a bucket list item of many years. I could not believe it when we were riding through the beautiful scenic countryside, carefully dodging chickens and navigating around horse drawn buggies carrying crates of fresh eggs. Coming around a bend to the base of a hill on our first long riding day, I happened upon the most colossal potholes in the known world. Of course, after six decades of being suffocated and strangled by the world political economy, the Cubans certainly had not had resources for infrastructure, especially as they used the meager resources they had, to first take care of people. The roads were tragically un-maintained. I gasped. It was only our first day of riding!

Embarking on that pothole scarred road, out of nowhere I was visited by a flashbulb image. Back before the pandemic when I drove to the office every day, I was routinely stopped by a traffic light, just as I was getting off the freeway. At that street corner was a little skateboarding venue, a little "park" of concrete, fitted out with sharp hills and walls, obstacles and vaults to jump, slalom type circles. Groups of adolescent boys (I never once saw a girl!) in baggy hoodies wildly flying round and round, jumping, crashing, rolling up the steep sidewalls, clearly having a blast. From the large graffiti on the walls, it appeared they referred to themselves as "punks." As I waited for the long red light to change, I loved to watch them, always thinking "You wouldn't catch me doing that!" Never!

Well suddenly that day in Cuba, the "light changed." Was it a neurofeedback "moment?" I don't know... Suddenly the Cuban potholes reminded me of those kids, who intentionally sought out the bumpiness, the vertical crashing and landing on their wheels upright, the slalom curving and dodging and missing each other, they do this for fun! Suddenly I imagined myself one of the "punks," having fun with the Cuban potholes. For the rest of that trip, I made a game of pothole dodging and jumping. Missing infrastructure, and prior trauma became my game: joy, fun and triumph!

Butterflies

Another symbol of transformation that I love,
are butterflies. However, I've never been fond of
caterpillars. I even have a terrifying childhood memory
from when I was three or four, of a park in New York
where there were so many squiggling caterpillars that
I literally could not put my little feet anywhere without
stepping on them. All I remember is just wailing
"Daddy, Daddy carry me!" I don't remember if he did,
just the terror. Anyway, those unsavory little creatures
somehow become butterflies. Which are beautiful and
I love them!

Interestingly, we call nervous excitement "butterflies"
in our stomachs. I remember Peter Levine's reminder
that in the body, excitement and fear feel very similar.
The Cuban word for potholes is "paches." Que Vivan
los Paches!

05

The Journey of 1,000 Miles: Hallucinogen-Assisted Psychotherapy for Trauma

In 2006 I made my personal discovery of local treasure Michael Pollan, courtesy of Terry Gross, the voice and brains behind National Public Radio's iconic program "Fresh Air." The dean of UC Berkeley's School of Journalism, Pollan was already a prolific writer, but my first encounter with him was through his then new Omnivore's Dilemma which has since become perhaps my favorite book of all time. It is a book about food (admittedly one of my favorite subjects!) but presented comprehensively including anthropology, history, culture and ethnicity, religion, nutrition, agriculture, ethics, psychology, art and science, wow! and even written skillfully with a poetic hand. I was stunned. And also amazed that for a bookworm like me, I had a rare if not first experience, of having one book actually significantly alter my view of more than one thing. I remember when I joined the throng of attendees at a (then free of charge!) public reading in the basement of Grace Cathedral early on a Sunday morning. I lined up with everyone else to have (an additional copy of) my book signed, I told Pollan, as I shook his hand, "You are perhaps the first author I have ever encountered in all of my bookworm years, who can actually change my mind!" Those words "Changing Our Minds," later became part of my professional logo. Of course I loved it when his 2018 blockbuster came out, and with the title How to Change Your Mind. He of all people would know. In 2018, my husband and I drove 50 miles each way and paid $20.00 a ticket for the reading. Still we were

lucky to get a parking space and two seats together. The crowd was mostly boomers, veterans of the Timothy Leary and Alan Watts generation, some accompanied by a subsequent generation or two. The topic of the book was evolving and expanding field of hallucinogenic substances. As ever, Pollan's writing is exquisitely personal, a style I find compelling, believable and inspiring. As with sourdough baking, home brewing, and even hunting, Pollan's first research subject was himself. He had the guts not only to experiment at the edges of the laws surrounding controlled and illegal substances, but to write about them.

Later that same year, I read somewhere that Daniel Siegel, the renowned attachment neuroscience researcher, infant psychiatrist cum Buddhist practitioner and teacher of mindfulness meditation, was studying the use of hallucinogens to address end of life issues. Perhaps most importantly, however, I

essel van der Kolk, the North Star of my
career was featuring at his annual Trauma
my decades long go-to for cutting edge
professional practice, full day workshops
est research in the use of psychedelics in
the treatment of PTSD.

Although I was no stranger to altering my own state, as many of us struggling to tame wildly dysregulated nervous systems, I quit everything in 1983 and became a grateful, sober endurance athlete. Considering these substances as a possible accelerated vehicle for healing, was mind expanding in itself. Attending that first workshop, although I had already read Pollan's book, was inspiring to say the least. Most significantly because seeing the video presentations of Iraq war veterans before and after a series of guided sessions using MDMA, and observing the transformation, was like watching the old time-lapse photography films where a caterpillar morphs into a butterfly in a period of moments before my very eyes. Sadly I recalled the one year, fresh out of graduate school, that I worked at the San Francisco VA. Back in the early 80's when we barely had a name for PTSD, let alone effective treatments, veterans of the Vietnam war suffered in their own personal never-ending war. Many of them looped in a revolving door-like cycle, in and out of the hospital, carefully not improving too much and having their benefit payments cut. The young men and women in the MDMA trials, in the mind-blowing videos, would most certainly go on to have lives and families, purposeful work and joy.

Since that first workshop I have attended the subsequent three including the virtual one during the Pandemic year. The progress in research and also FDA approval trials, is exciting. Psilocybin (magic mushrooms) LSD and Ketamine, are all also being carefully researched, including a to me local study, led by UCSF Nurse Practitioner Andrew Penn, on the use of Psilocybin for treatment- resistant depression.

Ketamine is now fully legal for use as a prescription medicine. And MDMA is edging up on approval for prescribed use for PTSD, with luck in the next year or so.

None of these medicines are or will be "stand-alone" treatments. All are to be administered by a trained, skilled and licensed health or mental health care provider. The treatment is defined and described as, for example, "MDMA Assisted Psychotherapy." Psychotherapy is the treatment, the medicines are components of said treatment, or "assistants" to the clinician. Similarly the clinician "assists" the journeying client. Training programs for how to assist are popping up like mushrooms in graduate programs around the country. I know in my area, they are exclusive and in high demand. Scoring a spot to even learn to be a guide, is growing to be increasingly competitive. I am cautiously optimistic and enthused by that, because it may mean the seriousness of the students, and thus growing public acceptance of the modality.

I do not see myself becoming a guide, much as I would love being able to add this remarkable treatment option to my armamentarium. The great task of the guide, apart from carefully crafted and executed pre and post psychotherapy sessions, is to be impeccably present. The guide might sit quietly for much of the six-hour journey, gently tracking, making observational notes and writing down whatever few words the client might say. In all candor I would have to say, I am not so good at the sitting quietly part, being much more inclined to interaction and reciprocity in my work. Thankfully there are already a number that are, some of whom have studied and trained with the true experts, indigenous people of both the US, and countries south of our borders. I am finding them and connecting with them so I will be well prepared with information and referrals.

I remember when I first heard about the Concorde jet, which could fly from New York City to London in 2 hours, 52 minutes and 59 seconds. For one who is not so good at sitting quietly for any length of time, that sounded beyond imagination. The work with hallucinogens may be the next "Concorde jet for PTSD, Developmental Trauma and Neglect!" I am hopeful! Meanwhile, Pollan has another brand new book: This Is Your Mind on Plants. In his inimitable style he expounds on his personal and then scientific explorations of Opium, Caffeine and Mescalin. Another highly recommended read. Happy Trails!

Trauma and Addiction: Reflections On My 38 Years

On June 15, 2021 I marked my 38th year of recovery from alcoholism. As is often the case I am stunned by the passing of the years, and also shocked to be reminded that I am that old! Oy vey! In this case I am profoundly grateful for the years, and the many hard lessons, and amazing blessings they contain.

In 1983 I was a profoundly depressed 28 year old, lost soul. Like most all survivors of trauma and neglect I was on an endless quest to find a safe place in the world; and beyond finding a purpose, justify my sorry existence. Like all other survivors my addled nervous system ricocheted ceaselessly between high anxiety and numbness; "hyper-arousal" and hypo-arousal" searching for the elusive moment of calm and ease, or at least relief. I was a distance runner, covering between 6 and 20 miles per day; I weighed 100 pounds (about 45kg). And each night, alone in my apartment in Berkeley, I drank a quart (roughly a liter) of straight Bourbon, Old Crow $6.95 a quart. I don't know if they still make Old Crow. That was my "go-to." It was what they called "rot gut" and I am sure it was! Then I would quietly pass out on the living room couch, with my journal or the latest book I was attempting to read, and my cat arrayed around me. A graduate of the University of California, and this was the best I could do? or so began the morning diatribe.

In the mornings, the face in the mirror horrified me. "What am I doing to myself?" I'd put on my sweats and go out to run. Those long stretches on the road, one would imagine I was thinking? I thought of nothing at all, it was raw flight. But I could not get away from myself. I would come home, somewhat sobered by sweat and the cool air of the wee hours, and make proclamations about quitting that day. Sometimes I would go to the length of writing a detailed plan of how I would do it, and then by evening, it would all begin again. I was like a rat on a wheel. We have all heard plenty of these boring "drunk-a-logs" as they are called in AA, and mine is not even colorful, racy, or funny. It was "pathetic" as I angrily told myself, and enduring.

Now looking back through a far different lens, it is a different story I see: it is the endless cycle of a traumatized brain and body desperately seeking "regulation" and calm, or at least relief, from the agony of unending flight. The alcohol was a momentary escape from that agony, moments at a time… until as they say, it wasn't.

The most salient lessons of these 38 blurring years, is that the drinking, the running, or it could be eating, love, shopping, whatever the obsession du jour, is yet another desperate attempt at momentary regulation, the ability to calm oneself down.

I learned just recently of old research using neurofeedback to treat addiction, that alcoholics literally use the alcohol simply to feel "normal." The measured "alpha" level, or the baseline nervous system calm equilibrium in the non-alcoholic control group was matched only by approximately 6 shots of hard alcohol in the alcoholic group. In effect, it took them 6 shots on average to get to "normal..." and that only briefly. As Sebern Fisher has so eloquently proclaimed, we are not really endlessly seeking a mother, but rather we are endlessly seeking regulation, and ultimately most of all, self regulation.

This is no "pink cloud" story. It did not get better overnight, by any means. I am eternally grateful and will always love AA, Alcoholics Anonymous, and no, one does not have to believe in God to benefit or to "fit in," in most fellowships. I went twice a day for the first two years of recovery: 6:00AM and 7:00PM and for those two years, those quiet hours in smoky church basements (and yes, in those days everyone smoked cigarettes!) were the only little islands of peace that I knew. I owe my life to that motley old organization. And my therapist Joan, yes the very one who inspired me to become a therapist after I saw that she really saved my life, recognized that it was the alcohol that kept me alive for those worst years of my 20's, until it started to and would have succeeded at killing me. Blessedly she had the wisdom to know the difference.

The Shape of Shame: Trauma, Posture and Coming to Tall

Way back when I was first training to work with couples, I studied with the renowned relationship expert and researcher, John Gottman. By now Gottman is about as familiar to the mainstream as a movie star, known for his 40 plus years of longitudinal data about what makes marriages "succeed or fail." In that early training, Gottman often referenced the work of Paul Eckman, who studied emotions.

Eckman's unique contribution was to discover the vocabulary of the face. He found through extensive and copious research and travel, a universal lexicon of facial and sometimes even body expressions correlating both cross-culturally and trans-historically to the specific emotions. This means that human beings (and some other mammals) configure their faces, and (with some emotions the body as well,) in a consistent, recognizable way, even identical way. In effect we do read and respond to the feelings of others with some accuracy. Thus there are silent (and often deadly) lengthy conversations, often outside of our awareness, transpiring much of the time.

This can be an advantage, however, and particularly with trauma and neglect of course, the complication is not the "read." Often the survivor is impeccably attuned to the subtleties of shifting emotion in others, obviously in the urgent mandate to pursue safety. The problem rather is in the interpretation. Survivors may quickly perceive and register anger, for example, but through the lens of their histories. So of course they may take it to mean "that it is anger at me" and then react to that. Sadly, many of our relationship nightmares are based on these redundant, mutual and usually escalating dynamics of mis-interpretation. And this is what can make the world of relationship a minefield, a waste-land, an elusive promised land or fiercely avoided "no man's" land for survivors of all kinds of trauma.

Eckman devised a system for learning to read emotion quickly, and I remember buying the sets of CD's (remember those?) and spending hours in front of the computer, flipping through the images of the many faces trying to improve my speed and accuracy at naming the corresponding emotion. Eckman went on to become an expert on lying and the ability to discern when an individual was lying. He became a high level consultant to the CIA and a sought after expert witness in high (and lower) profile criminal cases. Eckman himself struggled with his own anger, and I once heard him tell a remarkable story of how he worked with it. It would be too long to include in this blog but is retold in the book he co-wrote with the Dalai Lama, Emotional Awareness: Overcoming the Obstacles to Psychological Balance and Compassion. Well worth the read!

Shame

A persistent and agonizing emotional consequence of trauma is shame. Our understanding of this is even more pronounced, now that the trauma field has identified and named "moral injury" which is the category of trauma where the survivor has committed some heinous act, which was outside of their control. Veterans may suffer profound moral injury for atrocities that they were forced to perpetrate in the line of military duty. Medical personnel and first responders during the height of the COVID Pandemic similarly had to "let people die;" or choose who was to receive the ventilator when there were not enough to go around. But victims of violence themselves who did not in reality bring it in any way upon themselves, often feel responsible or as if they "deserved it" or did, in fact bring it on themselves somehow. Irrational as it may in fact be; they are haunted by that. Shame is an emotion that is most difficult to treat and alleviate, as it is so deep in the psyche and as we are now learning, the brain.

The Feeling of Shame

Many of us have at least heard the term Sensory Integration. For myself, before I learned more, I associated it to school kids with learning or behavioral problems.

It really has to do with connectivity and regulation between the various channels of sense perceptions, and other brain functions. We are all familiar with what are commonly thought of as the "five" senses: sight, hearing, smell, taste and touch. What we may be less aware of is the other three: introception, proprioception, and balance. Introception is the experience of what is going on inside the body, the sensation of a pounding heart for example, pain or tightness in the throat which may come with sadness and tears; the welling in the chest that might come with love or a burst of compassion. It also refers to pain, dizziness or numbing.

Proprioception is the body awareness of where we are in space, the demarcation between "me and not me" and physical closeness versus distance from other people and objects. I always wondered why I was so completely inept at catching a ball, or parking a car squarely between the lines, Balance of course, refers to equilibrium and solidity or grounded-ness.

Interestingly, the brain areas corresponding to body experiences are tightly connected to the limbic system, home of the emotions. And the limbic system is tightly connected to the prefrontal cortex, which is our "thinking cap:" executive branch. The prefrontal area regulates, not only cognition, but planning, agency, and sense of time, among many other functions. Just like the old song my dad used to sing to us "the shoulder bone's connected to the arm bone..." etcetera, etcetera down the skeleton, all these various functions are fundamentally interconnected. It makes sense that we might register (or not!) our various feeling states all kinds of ways. Some of us are very fluent at this, whether accurately or not.

When the primary experience is "incident" or shock trauma, the cataclysm of something that did occur, the individual might feel too much; when the primary experience is about missing experience or the overwhelming lack or what did not happen, the default might be to feel very little or even nothing at all.

One of the most pronounced and identifying features of a neglect history is the tragic poverty of mirroring. Mirroring is the reflection back from the caregiver of what the child is feeling, and perhaps attempting to express. Now at last we get to shame. When an infant looks up into the parent's eyes, and "I see reflected back, a loving image of me," that is when a sense of self begins to emerge and come online in the little nascent brain. With repetition, it becomes the default sense of self: "I am worthy, I am loveable, I am seen." When accompanied by an accurate read of my bodily and emotional needs, it is re-enforced. That is, if my hunger is accurately understood as such and gratified with food, my cold with a warm embrace or "blanky," my fear or loneliness with comfort and/or company, I learn not only that I am worthy, but with luck, learn to associate the need with its appropriate "remedy" and with luck, even learn the names for the complex of varied feelings. Sense of self ; self worth; the ability to identify, name, ultimately express feelings; and what is needed to fulfill or regulate them, all this is the product of accurate and sufficient mirroring.

No parent does it perfectly! In fact the attachment researchers tell us that the most attuned parents, who raise the most securely attached children, get the attunement accurately 30% of the time. 30 %! And all the rest is regulation and repair, which is how self regulation is ultimately learned.

In the case of shame, the poverty of mirroring means much of this fails to occur. The child may look up and see no-one or nothing there, an angry, fear stricken, hateful, troubled or disconnected face, and the result is confusion and anxiety. As the brain develops, the child will wonder why? Why am I hated, alone, not taken care of, cold hungry and afraid? The brain is ever in search of answers. Without a reliable source, we make one up: most likely, "I am worthless."

We default to cowering, hiding, searching for a way to be worthy enough: perfection? Helpfulness? Some way for compensating for one's "deficit?" The universal posture of shame is one of cowering, shrinking inward, pulling back, down and inward, almost as if to weather a blow. This unattractive and consistent body organization is a universal measure of shame. It is not sloppiness or laziness, not ugliness, but rather it is "Nature's Way of Telling You Something's Wrong…" Most of you are probably too young to remember that wonderful song.

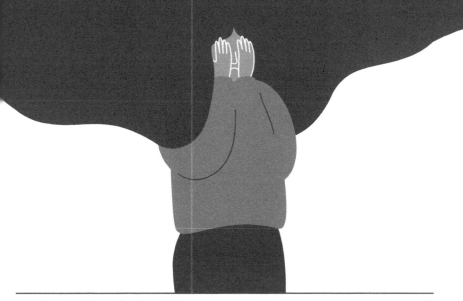

Working With the Posture of Shame

Working with the emotion and identity of shame is one of the hardest aspects of trauma healing. It begins so early and is so deep in the brain and non-verbal memory systems. Many of us have been at it for decades and it is still a work in progress! The method actors have long known however, that the deep interconnections between bodily, emotional and cognitive experience are multidirectional, or accessible via different access routes. They have found that if they put on, even feign the expressions that correlate to a particular emotion, the accurate emotion comes up, and perhaps even a personal memory. Or they might enter from the memory, or the body configuration and whichever way in, the skilled actor produces a believable replica or performance. Many survivors default to performance as a means of attempting worthiness, or a facsimile of relationship. I am not suggesting that! However a good body worker can help advance the progress of working with this complicated and hard to reach emotion.

So to sum up, a few suggestions, (and warning, none of these are easy to follow!):

· At the very least, try to stem and eradicate any shame about shame! It comes with the territory.
· Know that it takes time and work to change this!
· Remember that self-love is the learned experience drawn from having received and felt the love of another! If you lack the ability for self love, there is no shame in that! If is rather a point of grief!
· To just "stand up straight" may be very difficult! It maybe unsustainable, it may produce physical pain, it may be scary, it may feel very "fake" at least at first.
· Go gently.

A reputable form of body therapy with a skilled and knowledgeable practitioner can be an essential and expediting addition to healing.

Too Much of Nothing: Spotlight on Neglect

08

Trauma and Neglect

*"Now, too much of nothing can make a man feel ill at ease
One man's temper might rise while another man's temper might freeze
In the day of confession, we cannot mock a soul
Oh, when there's too much of nothing no one has control...
Too much of nothing can make a man abuse a king
He can walk the streets and boast like most but he wouldn't know a thing
Now, it's all been done before, it's all been written in the book
But when there's too much of nothing, nobody should look...
Too much of nothing can turn a man into a liar
It can cause one man to sleep on nails and another man to eat fire
Ev'rybody's doin' somethin' I heard it in a dream
But when there's too much of nothin' it just makes a fella mean
Say hello to Valerie. Say hello to Marion. Send them all my salary. On the waters of oblivion."*

– Bob Dylan

When I was a teenager, my first boyfriend Ted, was a serious photographer. I used to love to keep him company in the darkroom, in the rosy glow of the safe light watching the then complicated process of film developing. Sinking the eight by ten sheets in the tray of fowl smelling chemical he would shake it back and forth as slowly beneath the waves of the fluid an image would emerge. First blurry, it would gradually sharpen into focus until he determined the resolution was right, and would dunk it into the neighboring tray of fixer. For about 15 years I have been observing the shape shifting dynamics of psychological neglect in a similar way. Without the benefit of precise theory and formal research I am not even close to approaching the fixer vat. Rather this article offers the soft outlines of a profile of the "child of neglect" as it is evolving in my thinking. My hope is that you will join me in taking notice of a population that has too long been silent, invisible and ignored. What follows is the rough outlines of a developing theory and practice, including dips into the various vats that have served as input, influence and impetus for investigation. Although I have much nascent thought and practice regarding treatment, that will have to wait for a future article.

> Queried about their own past, they would respond, "Nothing happened to me!" What slowly began to take form was a vacuous wasteland of missing experiences. Precisely nothing had happened to them, although myriad developmental experiences and parental interactions would be required for a populated, lively and well-rounded childhood. Although they might acknowledge having been unseen, unknown or bored they are hard pressed to locate anything untoward in their histories, and often have very little memory or interpersonal memory at all.

The "child of neglect" first came to my attention by a side route. Long specializing in work with survivors of childhood trauma, I began to see them in couple's therapy, and I observed repeating patterns in the partners the traumatized seemed to bring. Invariably these partners were experts of the designated traumatized person's story, and mysteriously seemed to have no story of their own. Queried about their own past, they would respond, "Nothing happened to me!" What slowly began to take form was a vacuous wasteland of missing experiences. Precisely nothing had happened to them, although myriad developmental experiences and parental interactions would be required for a populated, lively and well-rounded childhood. Although they might acknowledge having been unseen, unknown or bored they are hard pressed to locate anything untoward in their histories, and often have very little memory or interpersonal memory at all.

They may however, be exquisitely focused and meticulously tracking all manner of details of the "other," whomever that happens to be, often a self styled or actual professional psychotherapist or analyst. They may have no idea of what they themselves are feeling (and they often don't), but possess an elaborate theory about your inner world, emotion or motivation.

Often these children of neglect have an appealing enough personality, but because they keep others at arm's (at least) length, they may appear aloof, diffident or cool. Because so much of their lives were spent in solitude they may appear to others to be self-concerned and unthinking about others which is often true. "Out of sight, out of mind" is an attachment survival strategy beginning in earliest childhood, well outside of awareness. They may think of themselves as thoughtful, not realizing that there may in fact be other subjectivities in the world and other ways of doing things beside their own. They may be baffled as to why their partners see them as rigid or controlling when they see themselves as being very rational and effective, generous and kind.

> Although one can strive to create an airtight existence free of human dependency, a dilemma is presented by sex. Although with sex, it is indeed possible to "do it all oneself" without the benefit of another, solitary sex is not the same. So how do children of neglect resolve this?

Not far under the surface there may be great anger, resentment, bitterness and cynicism. Again this is often far from accessible, highly ego distonic and disowned, and a therapy challenge to bring to light. It may also, however, be glaringly evident. A fascinating read is the recent autobiography of Rolling Stone Keith Richards, caricature of rebellion, rage and irreverence. His life is an illuminating illustration of the neglect profile, also highlighting the associated brilliance; endless efforts to populate the desolation with stimulation, thrills or escapism; and the typical overlay of concurrent significant trauma as well.

"No One Has Control" Three P's

Three signature character traits distinguish these individuals in relationship. I call them the Three P's: Passivity, Procrastination and Paralysis. Although they are definitely prone to anxiety, their tendency under stress is to freeze or collapse. A fourth P in the interpersonal matrix is Powerlessness. In relationship a typical and deeply resigned refrain is "I don't know what to do!" Or "There is nothing I can do," and the conviction about that is profound.

"Send Them All My Salary" Disavowing Interpersonal Need

The interpersonal world of these folks is marked by a rigid self-reliance, they adamantly do not need other people. Unaware, they may gravitate toward a political or spiritual perspective that re-enforces this or has them in self-sacrificing, care-providing or otherwise non-reciprocal relationship, or they may be remarkably autonomous or socially isolated. They may not even notice how reflexively they decline or reject any offer, devalue or "don't want" what is given. It is typically not needed, or the "wrong thing." Solitude or a world inhabited by the inanimate, non-human or impersonal (i.e. global or macro) animate is a more interesting, more comfortable or safer place to reside.

Although one can strive to create an airtight existence free of human dependency, a dilemma is presented by sex. Although with sex, it is indeed possible to "do it all oneself" without the benefit of another, solitary sex is not the same. So how do children of neglect resolve this? There are a number of variations. They may replicate their barren and wanting childhoods, by partnering with a sexually traumatized person unable or unprepared to gratify them, and have a sex life consisting of hunger, complaint, masturbation and preoccupation with the other's deficiency. One of my clients was 72 when I met him. He had spent years dragging his sexually traumatized partner to some of the most renowned sex therapists in the country. He knew her story like a book. It was only in therapy in his 70's that he began to discover his own. Finally working with his partner they began to have a reciprocal and ultimately even satisfying sex life.

Other neglect survivors resolve the conundrum through the use of pornography or professionals. With a professional, one need merely put the money on the bed stand and the danger of interpersonal need is handled. The distance is in place and it is safe to desire, to state clearly what is desired and even to be adequately satisfied. Sex may be lonely, alienated and shameful, but the problem of gratification is, thankfully, apparently solved, even if it creates secrecy or havoc in relationship. Similarly, pornography and alienated infidelity may be the "chosen" solutions. One can speculate about the Eliot Spitzers that leave us all scratching our heads and wondering "Why?" He seemed to have it all in place so why pursue pricey professionals?

Discovering in therapy that there may in fact be a place for their own needs and feelings in a live partnership that involves a sexual give and take may be a terrifying and ultimately transformative revelation. One client, a brilliant and highly successful businessman in his fifties had recently left his second long and sexless marriage. After thirty plus marital years of masturbation and what he described as compulsive pornography use, he was determined to have the sexual freedom that he had missed in adolescence and the sexual satisfaction he had longed for all his life. With high priced escorts, dominatrixes and non-commital encounters procured through casual sex internet sites, he let himself go, adamant that he would never marry again and that monogamy was not for him. He lived out this conviction even after meeting a partner whom he truly liked and who was truly available for sex, making his intentions very clear to her. He lived with her, and by agreement continued seeing professionals.

In therapy this client plumbed his history and began to piece together a desolate story. His father, a military man, was gone about 300 days out of the year beginning when my client was barely months old. His mother managed the burdens of household and parenting all herself, with both her son and then 11 months later his sister. He remembers years of time alone in his room reading, pondering profound existential questions and seeing little use for other people. Discovering sexuality had made him feel alive, if frustrated, and provided a first interpersonal impetus of sorts. Slowly in his fifties he began to develop a deep attachment to a partner truly committed to pleasing him both emotionally and sexually, but still adamantly held on to his convictions about "open relationship." Through in-depth therapy both individually and in couple's work with her he was amazed as he found himself wanting to marry her and even live a monogamous married life. It only came through the discovery of his own desolate story, and developing trust in his partner.

This is, due to the constraints of space, a hazy sketch of the neglect profile. Perhaps to continue the photographic metaphor, it is something of a "negative," highlighting the dark and hidden, even unsavory attributes of a population whom at first glance appears only attractive, successful, unscarred, uncomplicated and not in need of helpers like us. Rudimentary and incomplete as it is, perhaps this rough outline reminds you of someone you know.

"It's All Been Written in the Book" Assistance From Theory and Research

A number of important bodies of literature inform my developing thinking about this population. I am most interested in developing a deepening conversation about these and other theoretical and research wellsprings, and suggestions for more. Regrettably there is space here only to name these sources.

To me one of the most valuable of theoretical constructs is Attachment Theory and research. The Avoidant Attachment style provides a potent, preliminary template for the early experience of neglect, where the child is left far too much alone from earliest infancy. These babies may soon learn it is pointless to cry, because their cries echo into emptiness. They withdraw into self-containment and self reliance, although vicissitudes of attachment continue to elicit bodily responses of anxiety and depression. In the interpersonal world they lack initiative, follow-through, persistence and faith in another. They are prone to freeze and collapse, and they do not speak up.

Allan Schore and Daniel Siegel, in the groundbreaking work of interpersonal neurobiology, provide convincing and often heartbreaking data reflecting that the infant brain develops in resonance. For the first months and years of life, interplay between the infant's and the primary caregiver's right hemispheres, enable the emergence of essential functions and even structure. In effect, the parent's frontal lobes stand in for the infant's nascent ones for a time, as later the therapist's may be called upon to do. What becomes of the child whose brain resonates into a lonely vacuum too much of the time?

The field of Body Psychotherapy, beginning with Wilhelm Reich's Character Analysis offers Character Theory, a typology or alternative to traditional diagnostics. In that system the Oral or Self Reliant character typifies some characteristics of what I am calling the neglect profile. The most brilliant exposition I know of this protocol, is in the work of Stephen Johnson, most notably Characterological Transformation, the Hard Work Miracle. Johnson proposes that the ultimate therapeutic task of the Oral is to "get a voice, and get a spine," in the interpersonal, which although they may balk initially to hear it, resonates deeply with many of these clients.

The neurofeedback literature offers an illuminating account of the brain of the ADD and ADHD child, whose prefrontal cortex lacks stimulation and chronically under-fires. Like the experience of falling asleep at the wheel where we open the car windows, turn up the radio and seek stimulation of some sort to keep the heavy, hypnotic blanketing from taking over, the ADD or ADHD sufferer endlessly seeks stimulation to ward off the deadening of the sluggish brain. This is why the stimulant drugs are such a godsend to these individuals. Might it be the absence of resonance with another brain that originally spawned the low brain frequencies in the frontal lobes?

Valiant pioneers and researchers working to advance Developmental Trauma Disorder, a new diagnostic category for the upcoming revision of the DSM, are diligently studying children who fail to qualify for the diagnosis of PTSD, which effectively addresses the symptom constellation of adult war veterans. Classifying the experiences and missing experiences of these children will contribute to the body of knowledge about neglect and its consequences, and will create the diagnostic possibility for these children to get much needed help.

What else? How else might we advance the dialog about this neglected and quietly suffering population? I have so much more to say and learn. Perhaps you will join me. I observe that while these clients at first deny any identification with the experience of neglect or the designation, (and admittedly "child of neglect" is an impoverished or imprecise descriptor) those who do fit the description are often heartened and relieved that at last someone sees and takes an interest in them. Their partners definitely are!

Writing this got me thinking a lot about Ted. What a difficult relationship that was! His parents old world, working class Chinese immigrants left him alone a lot from his early infancy while they worked hard to run their flower business; all those years he spent in the dark by himself. I wonder what became of him.

The human brain, body, heart and soul are designed, wired and hell bent on connection. Without it, Dylan is spot on. "No one has control." We strive to fill the emptiness, with buffed up caricatures of ourselves, with artifice, with escape, numbing or with impassioned intention we manufacture something, be it destructive or creative to which we can resonate.

"There's something primordial about the way we react to pulses without even knowing it. We exist on a rhythm of 72 beats a minute. The train, apart from getting them from the Delta to Detroit, became very important to blues players because of the rhythm of the machine, the rhythm of the tracks and then you cross onto another track, the beat moves. It echoes something in the human body. So then when you have machinery involved like trains and drones, all of that is still built in as music inside us. The human body will feel rhythms even when there's not one. Listen to "Mystery Train" by Elvis Presley. One of the great rock and roll tracks of all time. Not a drum on it. It's just a suggestion, because the body will provide the rhythm. Rhythm really only has to be suggested..."

– Keith Richards

Waking Up to ACES – Neglect Edges into Awareness

Trauma and Neglect

The PTSD diagnosis only appeared in the DSM in 1980. To me that seems like an "augenblick" as my German mother used to say, the blink of an eye. I realize that many of my readers may not have been even a glimmer in anyone's eye in 1980. By now "trauma informed" is almost cliché, on everyone's lips, thanks in part to Bessel van der Kolk's block buster book The Body Keeps the Score, which everyone has read. If you haven't of course, you must, and you can find it in at least 10 languages if need be.

The PTSD designation was born out of the experiences of returning Vietnam veterans. Their devastating symptoms were stumping the VA as to how to help them. Many still wander around homeless and addicted, certainly in my area which is close to Haight Ashbury. The diagnosis was designed for young adult sufferers and pretty much only veterans could check all the boxes for diagnosis and treatment then.

At first we correlated the PTSD symptom profile with overtly physically violent life experiences. It later came to encompass traumatic events such as car accidents, and then domestic violence and rape. In the 90's violence against women and children came to be understood as traumatic the culture began to recognize the prevalence of these. Before that even physicians in training had no clue that they might be looking for evidence of these incest for example, it was not anywhere in their medical training.

In 2010, Ruth Lanius et al quietly wrote another epic, The Impact of Early Life Trauma on Health and Disease. It is another must read but most people haven't. In it Lanius and her co-authors widened the lens, to include a much wider range of life experiences that fit the definition and also the neuroscientific profile of traumatic experience; and also to include the medical impacts. In this book neglect shows up.

I have been studying neglect doggedly since about 1998. I am not a researcher so I have no evidence basis, just a treasure trove of anecdote, and my own personal theory and practice. Fortunately, now Lanius and van der Kolk and others are presenting the evidence and even the visuals to demonstrate it. And it is all still slow. It is still a rare therapist that recognizes neglect. The clients themselves usually don't, and because they are not aware that something "happened" to them, they wonder why they feel so bad, and therapists do too. Their missing story is about missing experiences, and it is difficult to see what is not there. I have found that clients who discover the neglect profile, and match their own feelings and patterns to it, have been so wildly relieved and grateful. That is why, I have been on a mission over these decades, to amass information and to share it.

In 1995, the mammoth medical group Kaiser Permanente, undertook a two-year study of what they called "Adverse Childhood Experiences" or ACES. They recruited 17,000 subjects, all drawn from their membership, which skewed the sample somewhat. The subjects were all employed and insured which implies a certain class affiliation; and so the researchers would not have expected to find what they did. The ACES encompassed among others:

· Experiencing violence, abuse, or neglect
· Witnessing violence in the home or community
· Having a family member attempt or die by suicide

Also included are aspects of the child's environment that can undermine their sense of safety, stability, and bonding, such as growing up in a household with:

· Substance use problems
· Mental health problems
· Instability due to parental separation or household

The results were astonishing. 61% of the subjects had experienced

At least one, and one in 6, had experienced four or more. Imagine if the study had included subjects of poor, unemployed and a wider range of backgrounds. And yes, neglect appears on the list. This was 1997, when the results went public. How come no one noticed. Now, like "trauma informed" which some of us were desperately trying to bring into the psychotherapy mainstream for years, the ACES are on everyone's lips. Why did it take so long? And how many survivors of childhood neglect, have slipped through the cracks un-helped and remained invisible all this time?

For at least 5 years van der Kolk and his research group has fought to get "Developmental Trauma Disorder" (DTD) into the DSM. The last edition rejected it. So there is still no formal diagnostic category to legitimize it, and also to facilitate insurance re-imbursement. To my knowledge, developmental trauma is not yet part of graduate school curricula.

Now the list of traumatic experiences continues to grow. We are coming to understand "Minority Stress" ie the continuing threat and insult to identity of racism and discrimination, and the danger of violence it often includes; and "Moral Injury" which is the shame and grief associated with having committed unbearable acts oneself. This was a feature of the Pandemic, when health care workers were unable to save patients from dying; or had to choose who got the ventilator and who died; and of course war veterans and first responders who commit heinous acts against other human beings. These are traumatic experiences that bring similar brain aberrations and symptom patterns to those that we recognize.

Thankfully the ACES study is coming to be known and considered, at last. Maybe Developmental Trauma will become recognized and understood, and clinicians will be learning about neglect. I'd like to see neglect come out of the shadows, and a vast population of invisible sufferers come into view at last.

10

George Floyd – Restitution, Apology and Forgiveness

On my mind

When I was barely more than a toddler, living in Manhattan, I learned a very big word: restitution. My parents, both survivors of the Nazi Holocaust, had not lived in this country too long. It was 1959. We lived in a large, old brick apartment building, where all our neighbors seemed to have numbers on their arms. I easily imagined that to be the norm, true of all people. One day, my parents received a letter in the mail. It said we would be receiving a small check each month: restitution. The German government was attempting to compensate Jews for the pillaging of possessions they had suffered. Of course they could not replace the 6 million murdered, but it was a gesture of reconciliation. It was the first I had learned of such a concept, attempting to repair broken trust or damage perpetrated. Although it was small consolation for my profoundly traumatized parents, it was still somehow gratifying and certainly much needed.

As an attachment theory-oriented therapist, I am still haunted by his cries for his mother in those last nine minutes of his life. "Mama, Mama…" As a somatic therapist who is regularly teaching clients about breath and a the calming power of intentional breathing, the words "I can't breathe…" the same words gasped by Eric Garner in a similar police murder in 2014, have gained a whole new traumatic meaning. What have we learned in this ensuing Pandemic year since Floyd's tragic death? Does anyone remember Eric Garner? Will anything be significantly different for the poor, disenfranchised and of color in our country and the world, or will this be just one more episode, like a traumatic flashback, that recurs and persists and continues to perpetuate pain and enduring dysregulation and dysfunction?

As a relationship therapist, I am constantly trying to teach clients and often couples the power and magic of apology. Most do not really know how, having never heard a meaningful apology for harm done to themselves, and also living as we do, in a culture of blame. Many even view apology as an admission of defeat, so it is a humiliation to take responsibility for relationship repair. If made at all, apology is tinged with a self-canceling defensiveness, and so have no impact at all. In a memorable episode of the long discontinued television program, Sopranos, when one character, Christopher, while under the influence of heroin, sat on and suffocated his girlfriend's beloved little dog to death. He shrugged his shoulders dramatically and exclaimed to his devastated girlfriend "Hey! I'm sorry!" Of course this had no meaning to the bereft young woman.

Eve Ensler, now known as "V" published a profound book that appeared in 2019: The Apology. Before that, I had found little literature of use on this crucial subject. For some years I have been gestating a book on the subject, which I still intend to write. But V's view on the subject was the closest to my own that I have encountered yet. In it, more than 30 years after his death, she writes the letter of apology from her viciously abusive father that she had always hoped and longed to receive from him, but never had. It is written in his imagined voice, and in chilling detail he recounts and owns what he did to her over decades. Without defending it, he also tells the story of is own trauma, which does not excuse the harm he perpetrated, but somehow makes sense of it for her. Oh yes: the intergenerational transmission of trauma. The book affected me so deeply, that I bought dozens of copies to give to friends, in my quest to spread the word.

Again, most of my clients, survivors of trauma and neglect, have never heard an apology for what they endured. And clients ask me, "Wasn't she doing terrible wrong? I am so angry! And I feel guilty that I am so angry. Could she just not help it? Was she just doing the best she could?" Both are true. But more importantly, how do we interrupt this insidious legacy? Restitution is a noble symbolic gesture, and certainly moves in the right direction, but it does not

go deep enough. Or it is effective but not sufficient. As Janis Spring Abrams, who writes eloquently about the trauma of infidelity, "cheap forgiveness" skips the depth of pain and rage, and fails to restore or create true, reparative intimacy. We need to fully experience the unsavory emotions for the apology/forgiveness to "work," and have impact.

I believe the way forward, besides transforming dysregulated brains with neurofeedback, and every way we can, is teaching the elusive practice of authentic empathy. A relatively recent concept, empathy only first appeared in the Oxford English Dictionary in the Nineteenth Century. It is still poorly understood. And it stands in contrast to the simpler, more familiar concept of sympathy. Sympathy is feeling compassionate and assumably understanding emotion on the other's behalf, but still squarely from one's own point of view. It is drawing on one's own reservoir of experience to imagine the feeling of the other, attempting to speak from that. One can still remain lodged in one's own narcissism, and even feel superior. Empathy however, is stepping if momentarily into the other's world, and working at truly feeling how it is for them. Not to agree or "give them a pass" so to speak, but rather to make sense of how this could have happened. V's father was the product of a horrific and unprocessed history. That by no means excuses wrong perpetrated! But rather makes sense of what is otherwise incomprehensible and unforgiveable. And forgiveness benefits, more than anyone else, the forgiver. V felt tremendous relief. It did not retrieve lost years, and the protracted storm of agony, or the thousands of helpful and unhelpful therapy dollars, but provided a sea change of direction. Granted, these perpetrators never chose to do their own work, which is part of what makes the questions complex unanswerable.

In cheese-making, the essential first ingredient is the starter culture, an interesting and unintended double entendre. The culture is an organic compound that stimulates or catalyzes the milk to "ripen" changing its chemistry to make it receptive to the agent of transformation, which miraculously transforms the milk from liquid to delicious solid. A certain amount of time is required for this magic to transpire, for the cheese to "mature." For the cheese-maker, patience is more than a virtue. I believe that empathy and the teaching of empathy, better yet, a culture of empathy, is an essential first step in breaking chains, of both oppression and intergenerational transmission of trauma and neglect. And of course continuing to stir the vat!